RIFT ZONE

RIFT ZONE

Tess Taylor

Red Hen Press | Pasadena, CA

Book layout by Mark E. Cull

Library of Congress Cataloging-in-Publication Data

Names: Taylor, Tess, 1977– author.
Title: Rift zone / Tess Taylor.
Description: First edition. | Pasadena, CA : Red Hen Press, [2020]
Identifiers: LCCN 2019038520 (print) | LCCN 2019038521 (ebook) | ISBN
    9781597097765 (trade paperback) | ISBN 9781597098625 (ebook)
Subjects: LCGFT: Poetry.
Classification: LCC PS3620.A979 R54 2020 (print) | LCC PS3620.A979
    (ebook) | DDC 811/.6—dc23
LC record available at https://lccn.loc.gov/2019038520
LC ebook record available at https://lccn.loc.gov/2019038521

The National Endowment for the Arts, the Los Angeles County Arts Commission, the Ahmanson Foundation, the Dwight Stuart Youth Fund, the Max Factor Family Foundation, the Pasadena Tournament of Roses Foundation, the Pasadena Arts & Culture Commission and the City of Pasadena Cultural Affairs Division, the City of Los Angeles Department of Cultural Affairs, the Audrey & Sydney Irmas Charitable Foundation, the Kinder Morgan Foundation, the Meta & George Rosenberg Foundation, the Allergan Foundation, the Riordan Foundation, Amazon Literary Partnership, and the Mara W. Breech Foundation partially support Red Hen Press.

First Edition
Published by Red Hen Press
www.redhen.org

ACKNOWLEDGMENTS

In writing and gathering these poems, I am enormously grateful for a MacDowell fellowship and for time spent as the Anne Spencer Poet-in-Residence at Randolph College and as Distinguished US Fulbright to the Seamus Heaney Poetry Centre at Queens University Belfast. Huge thanks to Sinéad Morrissey and the cohort of Queens University Belfast, and to Gary Dop and Laura-Gray Street.

Deep thanks to editors of the following publications where these poems appeared:

Alta: "Downhill White Supremacists March on Sacramento"; *At Length*: "Berkeley in the Nineties," "Song with Schist & County Line,"; *Copper Nickel*: "Song with Poppies & Reverie"; *Harvard Review Online*: "Found Poem: Pocket Geology"; *Kenyon Review*: "Apocalypto with Aquaria," "Song with Habitat Exchange," "Song with Sequoia & Australopithecus,"; *Literary Hub*: "February, Rain"; *Los Angeles Review of Books*: "In Olema"; *Mantis*: "Around the Hotsy Totsy"; *The New Republic*: "Song with Shag Rug & Wood Paneling"; *Poetry*: "Elk at Tomales Bay"; *The Tangerine*: "Loma Prieta 1989," "Punctuations and Wind"; *Tin House*: "Valley Girl & Paramount, 1988"; and *VQR*: "Aubade with Faultline & Broken Pipe," "Aubade with Redwood," "El Camino Real," "Escrow," and "I Gave My Love a Story."

The poem "Train through Colma" appeared on the San Francisco Muni as part of the 2020 Muni Art Project. Thanks to Darcy Brown and San Francisco Beautiful. The poem "Notes on a Diebenkorn" appeared in *The Eloquent Poem: 128 Contemporary Poems and Their Making* edited by Elise Paschen. The poem "Handgun & Tetherball, 1990" appeared in the anthology *Bullets into Bells: Poets and Citizens Respond to Gun Violence*, edited by Alexandra Teague, Brian Clements, and Dean Rader. The poem "Cardboard & Aria, 2011" appeared in the anthology *99 Poems for the 99 Percent*, edited by Dean Rader. The poem "Song with Shag Rug & Wood Paneling" appeared in the *Studio One Reading Series Chapbook* and in *Lightning Strikes II*, from the Dolby Chadwick Gallery. Thanks to these editors.

Enormous gratitude to early readers of these poems: Nuar Alsadir, Dan Alter, James Arthur, Michele Battiste, Nicole Callihan, Stephen Connolly, Forrest Gander, Lynn Melnick, Valerie Miner, Manuela Moser, Toni Mirosevich, Beth Ngyuen, Aimee Phan, Patricia Powell, Brynn Saito, and Dean Rader.

Thanks to Frances Kaplan and the staff of the California Historical Society.

Thanks to Bob and Brenda in whose good shade so many poems grow.

Thanks to Claudia Rankine for the prompt to write about blondness.

Thanks to Tom Panas for deep knowledge and Melanie Mintz for opening shut doors.

Thanks to the inimitable Ciaran Carson for guidance and generosity.

Thanks to Evan Bauer, Alejandra Detchet, and Jamie Valle for reading the fine print, and to Miriam Herrera for care across years.

Huge thanks to all of Red Hen, but especially to the wonderful Tobi Harper, for good wine and an even keel.

This was a labor of years: I send gratitude broadseed for community in which to grow.

Enormous gratitude to the Taylor, Clark, and Schreiner families for your great extended love.

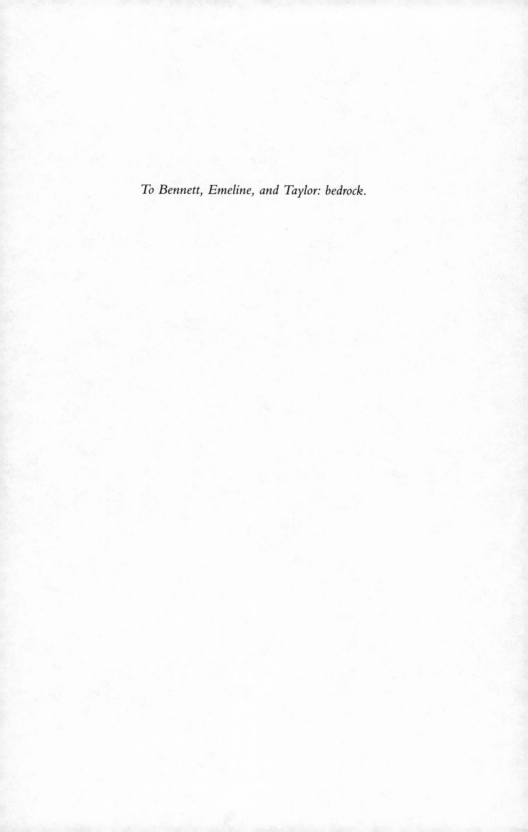

To Bennett, Emeline, and Taylor: bedrock.

CONTENTS

III

IV

V

RIFT ZONE

INTRODUCTION
TESS TAYLOR'S FAULTLINES
by Ilya Kaminsky

When Tess Taylor takes a large look at this place we call home, our North America, what does she see?

> Atop
> > the Earth's mantle, rock moving.
> > Continents are milk skin
>
> floating on cocoa.
> ("Preface: Pocket Geology")

Then, her lens focuses, and she sees San Pablo Avenue, which runs through San Francisco's East Bay:

> San Pablo, old trade route, widens there
> peppered by pupusa stands.
> Passes the crumbling mission and the corner
>
> where Donte, who my sister loved, was shot.
> ("Del Norte")

It is no accident that the perspectives in this book change from geology to microhistory with such incredible speed. One moment, we are to perceive the largesse of geological time. The next, we overhear a gunshot.

It was Chekhov who famously said, "If in the first act you have hung a pistol on the wall, then in the following one it should be fired. Otherwise, don't put it there." I have no doubt that Tess Taylor is well aware of this advice. For very early in *Rift Zone*, the readers will find these lines:

> No one explained the reasons
> > Dana found that spring
> to bring her brother's gun to school,
>
> triggers that led her to threaten
> > to *shoot you bitches*.

. . . .
I remember

Sierra Burch's thin legs running,
     a shrill voice yelling
          call the teacher.

In high-noon California sun
     Dana's palm was shaking—
her face tight with fear or anger.

In dream-time big men came
to cuff her & I heard her whimper.
     Saw her lean girl's body fall.
. . . .
     That day
we watched her disappear—
heard the big door shut,

the silence after.
          Decades floated
over all our bodies.
("Sixth Grade, 1988")

This silence in the presence of the gun shows Taylor internalizing a very American kind of violence—one that reverberates though the whole book. What do we find at the middle of perceived normalcy of a typical California suburb? Fear. The "silence" of the shut door. And, as often in Taylor's work, larger, almost geologic time enters: "decades float over all our bodies" (note: it is all our bodies, not just one).

What interests me most here is not that one gun, but how Taylor's lens allows us to see an aftermath. I am interested in her many investigations of American fear, especially in her ability to map it both in terms of geography *and* time: we watch the poet take the BART train through San Francisco watching "the old school crumbled in a landslide." At the same time, we see how generations of her contemporaries "disappeared / into our overpriced adulthood." I am interested, also, in how images of guns reappear in what should be a lovely California landscape. For instance:

> The man a few blocks over with his lettuces,
>
> raw twang & melanomic skin
> saw me walking with my infant son.
> He said *hey lady, keep in mind*
>
> *I have a gun. You can take my lemons if I offer,*
> *but steal 'em—bam—you'll know who's boss.*
> ("California Suites")

Then again, many pages later, we hear:

> Then once again someone is shot
>   at a school by a sniper by police in a movie theater
> . . . .
>   But you are lucky, so you try to feel lucky.
> By the numbers you have always lived
>
> in an apartheid state.
> ("Punctuations & Wind")

These echoes are no accident. The sound of "the big door shut, / the silence after" vibrates throughout the pages of this book, as years pass and "the decades floated over all our bodies." What is all of this motion? What is Tess Taylor doing here? In writing about the place in which she grew up and lives again, Taylor is, it seems, at home. But what *is* that home? Where does she live? She is mapping the landscape, yes. But her investigative act doesn't just happen in terms of geography or even in terms of history. She is also asking questions about our emotional relationship to this space we call home. It is also the to-pography of our emotions Taylor examines here:

> Bodies in space were revolution.
> Some of us were feminist & queer.
> Some of us wore wool sailor pants

& passed out at bad university parties.
Oh my god, that was embarrassing.
Some of us cut class to spend
days reading in the dank public library.
Alone in our aloneness we fumbled
with one another's bodies
in dim alleyways near City Lights.
Our revolution: under cherry blossoms,
reading Virgil.
("Berkeley in the Nineties")

With the turning pages, Taylor constantly shifts perspectives. But the place remains: California, as core sample, ethnography, representative history. The poet moves from personal detail to larger violence. She also moves from particulars ("blackberries choke the bike path; / schoolboys squall like gulls") to the largesse of hills and faultlines. We are in 2020 of our ultramodern moment, which nonetheless is inextricably linked to a 1933 when "some people from the Stege Church / lit up the hill / with their white enormous cross." Over and over, we are presented with a California of middle-class suburbia: "My parents renovated that old home," she says. "It is clean as a lobotomy." Cleanliness? Yes. But not exactly safety.

What's at play here is a very American kind of violence—done by time, or guns, or economics—which happens beyond or behind or even inside the façade of suburban landscape, unsettling the inhabitants who refuse to recognize it. The violence which middle-class Americans pretend not to see—though it is right in front of them (and us)—is perhaps at the root of Taylor's obsessive mapping. Is Taylor safe in her California suburb? Perhaps. But what does safety really mean in America in 2020? The answer to this question is uncertain, and this uncertainty vibrates through almost every poem in this collection. Taylor understands she is living at the edge of what might be a great gulf, in the face of what might be called precarity—of her own life, of the lives of people around her, of the geologic earth, of the planet as we know it. To simply *recognize* this in America today is no small thing. To *write* the kind of work that actually maps this gulf is special. The mapping here goes further than most: in fact, it extends to something scary—to the very bodies of her husband, daughter: "& nose your blowhole into flesh." Very beautiful, compelling poems for her family often involve verbs of motion and vocabulary of measurement. The poet chases the patterns and counts the stars:

> I only chase the pattern that I hear.

> Something I meant spins farther off.
>> And: You didn't die that awful year.
>> I haven't lost you yet.

> My love, I count the lucky stars.
>> I lie, rocking on your breath.
> ("Song In Which We Yet Sidestep Disaster")

This urgency—this foreknowledge of loss—points us back to the early pages of this book, points back to the first discovery of guns. We can almost hear again that "big door shut, / the silence after." The double-vision of Taylor's work, its constant need to shift and measure what is still hers, her poems' constant awareness that "everything we name / is disappearing" has a source. It has to do with her ability to overhear danger and see historic and cultural violence where others see a lovely American suburb. This is why perspectives shift so rapidly between scales (the domestic, the geologic, the political, the hypermodern, the ancient); is why the beautiful lullabies for her child in this book are so filled with sound and are "all vowel." In the end, this powerful book is the poetry of a mother who lives in a violent country which refuses to admit its own violence. But the poet sees it for what it is: she is not reconciled to it. Perhaps that is why there is such a piercing tenderness to these lullabies. Certainly, "Emeline at Six Weeks" is perhaps the best lullaby by an American poet that I have read during this decade. I think this beauty of sound has to do with the sober clarity of perspective on how things stand in America at this moment. The faultline here—the rift zone where Taylor lives—is on the ground between fear and tenderness. This duality makes the book so compelling, makes Taylor the poet for our moment.

rift zone ▸ *n.* A large area of the earth in which plates of the earth's crust are moving away from each other, forming an extensive system of fractures and faults.

—*American Heritage Dictionary of the English Language*, Fifth Edition, 2016

California is the product of a prolonged head-on collision between the leading western edge of North America and the floor of the Pacific Ocean as the continent overrode the ocean basin . . . the details are complicated but the broad picture is not.

—Roadside Geology of Northern California,
David D. Alt, Donald W. Hyndman

in the rift between what is going to happen and whatever we would wish to happen, poetry holds attention for a space

—The Government of the Tongue,
Seamus Heaney

PREFACE: POCKET GEOLOGY

Atop
        the Earth's mantle, rock moving.
        Continents are milk skin

floating on cocoa.
        A restless interior
        sweeps them along.

In trenches
                minerals decay—

at the core   landmasses

digest   themselves.

The crust does not move
in one piece   but in segments.

Mostly these carry
the continent with them, but sometimes

        continent
and mantle un-couple—

then blocks tilt
              like sidewalk

on unstable ground—

I

Whose fault
                our fault

& in the dream were marching

DEL NORTE

San Pablo, old trade route, widens there
peppered by pupusa stands.
Passes the crumbling mission and the corner

where Donte, who my sister loved, was shot.
Blackberries choke the bike path;
schoolboys squall like gulls or pigeons.

I rode the BART train with my Latin book.
Ayodele played college football,
but what became of Mynon Bigbee

Noah Zoloth-Levy Katie Bolton-Shmuckler?
The old school crumbled in a landslide.
We disappeared

into our overpriced adulthood.
The BART train hurtles past
raw schist and scar.

Stucco blocks repeat themselves
in sameness. In the corner
of my eye, another strip mall.

My mall: the one I grew up near.

SIXTH GRADE, 1988

No one explained the reasons
      Dana found that spring
to bring her brother's gun to school,

triggers that led her to threaten
      to *shoot you bitches.*
            We were nubbly, by the morning glories—

hadn't scattered different ways.
      We were playing tetherball.
I remember

Sierra Burch's thin legs running,
      a shrill voice yelling
         call the teacher.

In high-noon California sun
      Dana's palm was shaking—
her face tight with fear or anger.

In dream-time big men came
to cuff her & I heard her whimper.
      Saw her lean girl's body fall.

This year I found a photograph:
      Dana and her friend Mynon
mug for my frame.

Mischievous grins
split baby cheeks: ponytails
bustle in the wind.

It came back like a rusty fountain,
a smell of chalk & sixth grade funk.
We were learning

fractions. That day
we watched her disappear—
heard the big door shut,

the silence after.
                    Decades floated
over all our bodies.

        All the schools
have drills for guns now.
None of this names how it feels

to look back thirty years & find
this odd remainder.
Bright and on the verge of life,

as if we are yet unhurt:

            There's Dana smiling.

SONG WITH SCHIST & COUNTY LINE

The town of El Cerrito, CA, pop. 23,000, was first incorporated as Rust,
after the name of one of its most prominent nineteenth-century Anglo farmers.

i

The little hill exists, the one
the town was named for. It is
a huge real hill, not "Lakewood" or "Happy River"

where the name points to a thing that never was
or is so fully paved
no one can find it now.

Our real little hill
looms just south of town.

ii

Before this town was town it was
    "unstable real estate,"

the last Castro inheritors
    of a Spanish land grant

locked in US land dispute.
    Their great-great-grandfather arrived

on the De Anza expedition. They claimed the land
    for Spain, then Mexico. They

    built their adobe hacienda
    in the shadow of the hill, near

a radiolarian outcrop
    of Jurassic limestone

on windswept treeless grassland
    here when mastodon

wandered to the Farallones.
    Their house faced the glittering span

we now call the Golden Gate.

iii

After this stopped being Mexico
the Castros traded land in parcels

to pay off American lawyers.
Japanese immigrants acquired

wide plots for building nurseries
along the streetcar line. They took roses each day

by ferryboat to San Francisco—

(*had to purchase land*
                under the names
                of their American-born sons).

iv

there were also
chicken farmers

greyhound racetrack   mobsters
retired prospectors   & escapees

from the 1906 earthquake,
Italians & backyard vineyards

& (I hear) a tunnel
       under Central Avenue

where gangsters cached bootleg liquor
(*never confiscated during Prohibition raids*).

Hillbillies played the Six Bells
                  (*now the Burger King*).

They called our town *Stege*, then *Rust*.

v

Some people from the Stege church
lit up the hill
with their white enormous cross.
Easter 1933, they burned it for the Klan.
    (I only lately learned this—
        latest in the line of histories
            they don't teach / I didn't know—)

                    —all of us were always perched
                        atop a Ring of Fire—

Developers slapped up houses
& quarried blue-schist hillside
& used upthrust seafloor
for constructing modern freeways;
& Dorothea Lange traveled from Berkeley
to photograph migrant workers
& the Portuguese farmer Balra
sold his ranchero up the hill—
it became split-level tract homes
the Japanese were not allowed to live in
"nor any person not of the Caucasian race,"
        the titles said.

                  —great moving fissure where the earth
                      destroys and births itself—

vi

In Richmond, the ship industry was booming
& workers from the South traveled
by train & Model T
across Depression valleys—
Okie & black—all here to work—
(only some allowed to buy
          the bungalows of California)

By then it was unclear
                    where the many members
of the Castro family were.
                    They had mostly scattered.
Unclear if by then the redwood
                    on the streambed
in what became our backyard
had been planted. Now the hill
was bowling alley, *Wild West Gun Shop.*

                              —it also tears—

vii

Dusty, crumbling, facing the Golden Gate
the hacienda stood as it had stood
as three nations claimed it.

Arch corridors peered
past live oaks to the bay.
A few historians told me

how it became a brothel
in disrepair
& just as preservationists

began to try to save it,
it mysteriously burned. Overnight
some developer

slapped up the boxy *Plaza*—

viii

They plunked a BART station down
    on the lumberyard.

The racist codes lived on
    in escrow files.

A few families did
    return after internment.

Unbuilt lots still gape
    along the Avenue.

On the hill, the Lions
    light their hot white cross at Christmas.

Beneath it now we all
    can buy cheap wine at Trader Joe's.

The local historian says
    he does not know about the Klan.

Hidden in a cave, Ohlone petroglyphs.
    In our city hall: One dense adobe brick.

BERKELEY IN THE NINETIES

again for C. & J.

Too late for hippie heyday
& too young to be yuppies
we wandered creeksides & used bookstores.
There were still so many movie theaters.
Our parents marched against the many wars
& fed us carob chips. We foraged
in free boxes for old wrap skirts
but had absorbed consumerist desire,
& also longed for new J. Crew.
There was no internet yet & so we listened
to Steve Miller Band on repeat
& cut geometry to skinny dip
in the Essex Street hot tub.
We knew the code, just as we knew
to disapprove of America.
We walked out of high school
after Rodney King. We helped our mothers
shop for bulk oats at the Co-op.
We felt we could & couldn't
solve it. We could say *systemic racism*
but couldn't name yet how our lives were implicated.
We drove our grandmothers' Volvos up Marin
& watched the spangled world
from Grizzly Peak. We climbed Mount Diablo
in spring rain. We learned
the meaning of the word hegemony
but thought the word itself was *hegemonic*.
We got high to the patter of the windchimes.
When we missed our friends
we wandered to the farmers market
for bruised peaches. Bruised peaches were
our kind of revolution. There was not internet yet & so
we made elaborate cutout flyers to invite
our friends to picnics up at Codornices.

Bodies in space were revolution.
Some of us were feminist & queer.
Some of us wore wool sailor pants
& passed out at bad university parties.
Oh my god, that was embarrassing.
Some of us cut class to spend
days reading in the dank public library.
Alone in our aloneness we fumbled
with one another's bodies
in dim alleyways near City Lights.
Our revolution: under cherry blossoms,
reading Virgil. One of us made red
mushroomy kombucha. One of us
taught the others to eat burdock.
The burdock eating didn't really take.
Some days we paid the toll
for people behind us
on the Richmond–San Rafael Bridge.
At Steep Ravine howled Whitman at the sea.
Most days, we were a crumbling outpost. Nearby
the street preacher, Paul of the Pillar,
spoke in helter-skelter baritones from
liberated air on the Cal campus.
We too believed in liberated air & some nights
bought Paul sausages at Top Dog.
Under the Campanile, we discussed
how Ginsburg was a sellout now because he posed
for Gap ads in wide-legged chinos.
Chinos were not the revolution.
Trigonometry was not the revolution.
We memorized short poems by D.H. Lawrence.
We were quick fish who read
Gary Snyder in someone's dad's Mendocino cabin.
Some of us climbed ferny gullies

on winter solstice & got topless.
Decorated each other in white reindeer lichen.
Recited the *Tao Te Ching*. Had sex on a cliff.
Reindeer lichen was the revolution.
Our new breasts in rain were revolution.
We craved transcendental revelations,
the radical & burning future:
We lobbied for condoms in the high school bathrooms
even though the bathrooms needed toilet paper—

THREE DREAMS, 2018

i

Whose fault
                    our fault
& in the dream we were

            still marching somewhere
            in fog, in acrid smoke.

We'd wait out apocalypse up in the hills.
We'd summon the spirits of coyotes.

There was no middle anymore
            it was a mudflat flanked by peaks

                    superrich

                                    encampment—

                & oysters braved the tidelines
cleaning the bay out in their guts.

You must always live on the brink said Breton
            & so the brink cut through our backyards.

Most days it felt like nothing
            we didn't think of the street as old seafloor

except when earthcrust would snag
                    the foundations
                            of expensive houses

                suddenly upthrust
                        like revelation—

ii

Sometimes you glimpse her
the girl she was in free-box flannels

she was you & you were radical
ready for change & feeding on used books of poems

Maybe history is already over
said Fukuyama then   but so much happened:

you're here now   that ghost is lithe and strange
as the deer who bounded

in front of Monterey Market
                uncomprehending

iii

I live on faultline which most days feels like nothing
except in sidewalk crosshairs

streambeds where schist
& bay leaf seep into the sea.

Earthteeth, guzzling serpentinite.
When they interned families from my town

they sent them first to camp on a racetrack
then into an arid valley

torn between dry mountain ranges.
What was before comes back again.

I retrace so many fragments:

what did I ~~not~~ know

                              was already happening

SONG WITH SHAG RUG &
WOOD PANELING

My parents renovated that old home.
It is clean as a lobotomy.

The cracked linoleum's erased.
New hardwood floors are gleaming.

Gone are gold shag rugs the shade
of California August,

on which I lay beneath the dust motes
studying the drift of genome, species, phyla;

gone the shameful faux-wood paneling,
dark embarrassment of my teenage years.

They've added a back door to the kitchen
where night after night I fought with my mother—

      I, who spent a decade sending hatred
toward a glittering asbestos ceiling,

have only a distant dump to hate;
the settling of old carcinogens.

My ancient vehemence is confounded
by brightly lit new silence,

emptiness beneath the open vaulting.

SONG WITH SEQUOIA &
AUSTRALOPITHECUS

Limber pine, marbled godwit, diffuse daisy, stonecrop,
   I was learning your names—
then heard Bennett waking.

    On today's pajamas he wears dinosaurs.
He does not know dinosaurs or that *pajama*
   is Hindi via the British;

or that this tree is a paleolith,
   or that this state was Spain.
Some year I'll tell him:

    What is life for but explanation?
Now he wakes under a tusky mammoth.
    His arms flail & he reaches

for a tree branch to keep from falling.
    (He lies on the ground.
    There is no limb.)

Moro's gesture: vestige of monkey self.
   My primate grips me in new human skin.
I rock him near blooms labeled *sea thrift*.

    Each body cradles its own conservation.
Each body bears forth the enormous dark chain.
   We only half-grasp what we inherit:

In caves the first humans played
   parts of the Doric scale on their bone flutes
do re mi fa vibrating over eons.

Our ears cock
                              to old tones.
Scientists believe that our wrist bones

          tell us which Australopithecus
          was our progenitor.
O dinosaur, O Australopithecus.

          I rock my wrists, I grip my son.
I might say *Earth thrift, life thrift,* or *tongue thrift.*
          Might say *word-crop: pajama: Empire.*

          Today I revert by instinct

to glottal percussion.
                              I coo & croon.
          Air blows

          through my hollows.
I telescope song-shape
into vibrating chambers—

into his ears, fresh gills of this air.

II

The last mangled slice of sea floor sediment and last shattered masses of ser-pentinite were added to the Coast Ranges perhaps eighty million years ago.

Some of these breach faults are well known and precisely mapped, but others are not.

Years of geologic work will be needed to unravel and finally assemble all the stray pieces of the San Andreas puzzle of faults.

—Roadside Geology of Northern California

SONG WITH PNEUMONIA & TELEMANN

Mountains lost in clouds.
        Woman in roadside rain.
Refinery silos, tumoring the hill.

The bay heaves daily systole / diastole
        through blasted estuaries;
I follow the path De Anza charted,

now freeway, to the hospital.
        Taylor inside, week three, a mystery—
"all diseases partly drug resistant"

says our brusque nurse.
Terrifying illness, unexplained.
On my iPhone, a Telemann sonata,

arpeggios, progressing scales.
In Taylor's lung, liters of yellow fluid.
Bennett says *caboose*; says *knuckle coupler*.

Says *buckle*; *puzzle*; *horn*.
Bennett feels untainted joy in engines,
but when I park in San Francisco

& chart my breath beside the beeping
        monitor my love is hooked to
I read the toxins in our tide.

Today, tubes, a fifth antibiotic,
        my husband struggling for his pneuma,
spongy tubules in his lung's great cloud.

The scales grow furious. The song is cycling.
　　　When did it begin, this wild crescendo?
At the seventh antibiotic they'll give up.

Doctors take him for another test.
　　　Redwoods can drink fog.
Their needles sip the numinous.

Redwoods make their own groundwater.
　　　My love is elsewhere, being scanned.
I dream the limbs of old-growth forest.

Beyond my perch, my Telemann,
　　　someone is responding, not responding.
Each engine, each mortal machine.

Now, another body carted in.
　　　I perch on this electric bed.
Biotic, antibiotic: I am rocking.

I dream that I can be my husband's fog:

I dream our lungs as cloud as tidal skein—

CALIFORNIA SUITES

I. Rainy Season

Season of mud, of swollen gullies,
storms lashing off the Pacific, flinging
wet across our solstice months.
We call this bitter damp the winter
but it is different than rosy cheeks or blizzards
or catalogs of kids in reindeer sweaters:
Our winter turns the hillsides emerald.
Suburbs reveal thoughtless paving; drains
gargle now where salmon spawned.
Plum blossoms eddy
next to candy wrappers.
Between storms, the light is mercury.
Huge wet sets hillsides careening
hurtling down what faultline just thrust up.
Now ferns glisten, redwoods blacken.
Now cold buckeye seed & lemons come.
In rain, streets grow riverine
ferrying our cargo to the ocean.
O cold spray & green reclaiming:
In you, we are all tributaries.

II. Sempervirens
—California Redwood

We have no old cathedrals here
except for redwood groves
that wait in parks
behind brass plaques. Signs
date the oldest to Columbus or
William the Conqueror;

new roads wind to suburbs
that replace them. The plaques
are odd, as if we lack
another way to hold in mind
vast presences—
                             eons

passed in widening,
hosting murrelets & owls.
They carve the real estate
of centuries. They calendar
the former climate's fires.
White settlers

cut them down
& made them cheap
& turned them back
into a luxury.
Now we stroke their burls
with short-lived hands.

They model wise economy.
Each ring is still a living record;
a transitive, ongoing,
giant conjugate for *being*,
rhyming out
inside its own slow time.

They widen now
as ripples do
on deep & pooling streams.

III. El Camino Real

The corridor parades its stucco newness.
What king was it that built this highway?
Jornaleros in wide bucket hats

wait for hire beneath the on-ramps.
Blocks fill with retirees from somewhere colder.
Chapped garages hold canned food & water

hoarded against sure disaster.
In sharp heat, the lava gardens bleach.
The man a few blocks over with his lettuces,

raw twang & melanomic skin
saw me walking with my infant son.
He said *hey lady, keep in mind*

I have a gun. You can take my lemons if I offer,
but steal 'em—bam—you'll know who's boss.

IV. Escrow

In every sale, a list of ways
your home could be destroyed.
Flood, earthquake, fire.
Your house may end in mudslide,
be damaged by a rain of golf balls;
you may live downwind of poison breezes
off oil fields, refineries, or croplands.
You must assert you have
considered agricultural toxins; the risk
inherent in tectonic plates.
Signing on the dotted line allots you
a postcard plot of Golden State. Will
it be cancerous? God-willing
not to you. Your new house is younger
than your mother.
At your bottlebrush,
native hummingbirds.
Behind them, two huge redwoods wait.
In redwood years, these trees
are babies. They overlook
your fragile real estate.

DOWNHILL WHITE SUPREMACISTS MARCH ON SACRAMENTO

High in the Sierra
green summer aspen

whisper to the lake.
The snowpack glitters.

Over the passes
Winnebago thunder

      out of the wide red flats of Nevada.

Huge crooked knuckles,
the dark screes loom.

Deep in the roadbeds,
the bones of the Irish

& Chinese workers
whose lives were pitted

against one another
to drive down & down

the price of their labor
—who shattered their bodies

      dynamiting these crossings—
blaze in their graves.

SONG WITH HABITAT EXCHANGE

Calmada, Calmosa, California, Mar Vista,
        Ocean View: In duplicate languages, street names proffer

synonymous peace. The billboard hawks
        "affordable luxury"—the building is derelict

        no ocean view no sidewalks parks gated
even these nature paths blazed by oil rigs

even this trail a scar from fuel excavation.
        I am pregnant again: The dust makes me cough.

Cool mornings I still hike the arroyo:
        The plants here are replacements of plants removed elsewhere

"habitat exchange"—stand-in ecosystem—
                for gnatcatcher, sumac, eucalyptus

scarred elderberry, shimmering mule fat.
        Arid

crackle in the mud rat's nest.
I pause near the tunnel: The baby kicks.

                Black sage blooms in a dry inflorescence;
the toyon is a distant cousin of the rose.

Buckwheat bush, sunflower, endangered roadrunner;
I hear the *cheat cheat* of a towhee.

Whatever can wait waits for uncertain water:
        The mod suburb beyond us

crumbles already.
    I watch an unmoving freeway.

Stalled tankers grit particulate air.
    Now, from the ridgeline, I glimpse the sea.

YEAR OF DROUGHT & PROTESTS

Tonight the train shuts for another death.
Jumper: third this month,

"a rash of copycats," they say

in this hard year of drought & protests.
Beyond us, persimmon sunset.

Horizon, bright as abalone.

Traffic throb on freeways, mussel dusk.
From the station now slow cars

process. A hundred station-goers, all rerouted,

disperse to homes or cabs or friends.
Deep inside these shadows

some collapse. Absent
synapse—tendon—self.

Unrecoverable hub.
We each hurry on, not looking.

Dark is falling. All our taillights throb.

CARDBOARD & ARIA, 2011

& after the vermillion opera curtain
rose on Giovanni raping
the tiny distant woman on the stage,

       we drank champagne at intermission
& exalted in the opera's country dance.
We saw the soprano's elaborate

improbably choreographed
       re-seduction of her lover . . .
                             (*fa la haa eeee*)

& left the Opera House to head
down Market Street. The leathered skin
of that year's men was peeking

out from boxes pitched as tents.
The camps were already grown & growing:
I heard again the aria, *REPENT.*

Down the street, protesters
held signs: *We are the 99 percent.*
By sheer dumb luck we had a home to go to.

We rode a train to wine & soup & bed,
but in the early hours an earthquake heaved
our bungalow on its soft-story floor.

I dreamed it as the Comandatore's fist
cuffing us just at the gates of hell.
I felt aftershock

          & cold fog drifting.

Awake I wrote

        the dream is not a myth

wanted *to shake*

                            wanted *to be shaken*

AROUND THE HOTSY TOTSY

1

Nights, the young crowd, hipsters mostly.
By day, old bartender old men.

2

Coastline boxcars thrum:
Nights we wake & hear them pick up speed

a slow rag played out sad
then faster   wild harmonica

blown long   *cloudsong*
along the crooked elbow, California

they claim the coastal route
for freight for trade

3

Coyote bush & buckeye hunker:
On Chevron land now many squatters camp
perpetually inside the rail-yard swamp—

refinery, chaparral, and foxweed;
tents & barrel drums.

4

Once this was a mussel-gathering spot a midden
once a farm a wartime factory
who lives here now paves paths with cardboard;

& if you leave your trail by accident
you find a piss-stained mattress, jetsam needles.
Between poppies, rusted box spring.

Half a greeting:

                                        -LCOME.

FEBRUARY, RAIN

1

Dawn, after the hoped-for downpour.
    Droplets beaded in the sage.

2

On hills, ruts revert to streambed:
    Thistle-blue, the sky in rivulets.

3

On damp
fallen leaves, bright fungal blooms—

4

Live oak cradles winter sun: Satsuma.
Winter clouds—swift coho salmon—

5

Along freeways, pans & garbage.
    Fragile line between expensive & discarded.

A screen, rotating advertisement.
A camp: three tents, two bicycles.

6

On this road, backlit coyote:
    Quick illuminated trickster god—

7

At home: Absentminded,
under storm. Symphonic

crash, then silence.
Everything is gleaming, gleaming.

We prime ourselves to forest atmospherics.

8

On the mountain now mossy live oaks
twist, softening our hills.

      Druid, *draoidh*—some greenish
      Welsh or Celtic god

lodged in a latter Spanish colony.
After rain: white steeple, green behind it.

9

The light might be the Philippines or Goa.
Little mission church on a green hillock.

10

O white sanctuary gleaming:
      You trail all your bloody histories—

VALLEY GIRL & PARAMOUNT, 1988

I'm twelve, for the first time ever watching
Earth Girls Are Easy with Rochelle B.
at the Paramount in San Francisco

in whose deco dark we flicker into
the enormous San Fernando Valley
as maze of split-levels

freeways turquoise pools.
A pod lands. A blue alien seduces
Geena Davis the high-cheekboned hairdresser—

she squeals he is so furry & so other
but she soon reveals his nearly human beauty
when she shaves his blue & alien hair.

Like *omigod!*
               he's *actually* Jeff Goldblum!

Wait: Did they blastoff to another moon?
California: Asteroid & star.
California: Futuristic planet

on which hairdressers danced & sang
songs about their blondness
Because I'm a blonde I don't have to think

I talk like a baby & I never pay for drinks—
Easy: blonde as plundered sunshine
(*Because I'm blond Bee-eL-Oh-eN-D-eee*)

Nazi ideal in a parched valley.
Little sex-show song: white-blonde ditz song,
please harass/date me song.

Easy: I loved it so much, like trying on
my own pink training bra.
Melissa K. & I learned to lip-sync it

for the sixth-grade talent show
jiggling our arms & legs & also pouting
   I don't have to worry about getting a man/

   If I keep this blond & I keep theeeesee tan . . .
Absorbing watermelon glister
the way some jellyfish or squid

grow coterminous
with phosphorescent cells
that make them bioluminesce,

we grew in symbiosis
with fucked-up desire.
   Cause I'm a blonde don't you wish you were me?

That year I would refuse
my lunch in search of bonier hips,
use my hunger to propel

myself towards some imaginary center,
warped magnetic field that sucked
as I drew nearer,

amplifying its desires.
I wanted what it was / was sex / was power
was hyped-up preteen musk potent as

the American myth of newness
or the bloody hills of California—
I was an Earthgirl: I lived in a Valley.

I kept reciting just a little further

the toxic playbook where I learned myself—

HANDGUN & TETHERBALL, 1990

Portola Middle School, they called it.
PMS, we said, feeling awful
packed together in our teenage sadness,

finding out the colors of our skins.
In long hallways, in classes of forty-two students
we learned codings, locker numbers, gangs.

Mrs. Nagsake Mrs. Theissen Mrs. Mitchell—
Mr. Hall—Polyester, acid-breath:
Our district skidded forward, bankrupt.

Lunches soured in their plastic,
busses idled in blaring heat.
Even so that year we still belonged

a bit to one another's childhoods
to years we'd shared together and not yet
to wars waged in our names

& to racism poverty & privilege
though they were carving us/we were already carved.
We ran together punching tetherballs.

No textbooks   teachers   toilet paper
hull from which some of us headed
immediately to prison

some to private school or to Nation's Burgers—
                    Jabraun, the long-lashed boy
                    who taught me how to use a combination lock

& said I was pretty for a white girl
shot the next year—dead three decades.
I conjure up his raspy whisper

his brown eyes flecked with hazel sun.
O those years of sweaty suffering:
            We sprayed our bangs & danced to Boyz II Men,

& fumbled still towards one another,
running at the tarmac of our lives,
towards some impossible flight.

Brash laughter ricochets
out to the future.
I lug my dumb survivor's grief.

O they are tearing down that school:
It was always in a landslide zone.
Perhaps it will be returned to hillside.

            Perhaps someone will plant
the hillside with wildflowers
which the legends say were also blooming

when Portola, *Conquistador*, came.

NOTES ON A DIEBENKORN

—Cityscape 1, 1963

How in him the light is primary
the high hard sheen of Berkeley,
eucalyptus hitting walls—

How his trick is catching
some refraction off the water,
beveled salty mirror

forging afternoon.
The copper's shifty now
enough to tempt the fog in—

chartreuse & mineral asphalt
& a turquoise line—
foregrounded intersection

of gray maybe freeway

violet window // red streak

mainlined from Matisse—

ecosystem

constellation

map at height or speed—

Afterlife or foredream,

all this blurred onrushing:

Bright off-center longing
I always sense as home—

III

Each region has its own geologic style that permits some rocks to form and prohibits many others. We try to point out the possibilities within each region to give a general idea of what to expect.

Hopefully you will be able to tell for yourself what kind of rock you have.

—Roadside Geology of Northern California

APOCALYPTO W/ AQUARIA

Touching an urchin
in the reflecting pool,

Bennett says *salt*.
Urchin, I say. *Anemone.*

Each day he sings new syllables.
Anemone alemony amelony a melody—

We watch jellyfish, volutes in the tank.
Jellyfish thrive in many waters,

also in the face of vast pollution.
Next: endangered alligators;

cloudy octopi, one solo turtle,
back venerable as Aztec masonry.

Bennett says *tortuga*. Each day
his bestiary grows.

Still everything we name
is disappearing:

Zebra, hippopotamus, rhinoceros.
Soon I'll also be explaining

how each word each marks
a half-lost species:

O exotic & endangered letters.

BREACH & WAKE

Daughter, sprog, fresh Odysseus,
amniotic, blue velella.
Kelpy grasper, baffled by light.

Your cry is the clatter of gulls.
Our limbs are your octopus.
We're foggy, adrift.

Days crash & sail over.
Double-hearted, many-chambered,
we grow creaturely.

Then you, half-blind,
breach & wake, laborious porpoise,
& nose your blowhole into human flesh—

SONG WITH POPPIES & REVERIE

Thirty years later, my body grown.
Flickering signal economy, also fire poppies
in the lava garden. Clumsy

arthropods, fat pollinators.
Equal in mystery: I am a mother.
What does it mean to belong to July?

Blackberry, thistle, nectarine shadow.
How have I survived even this life?
At street corners sometimes

       time hauls me under
like the stone guzzle
where the land's crust

       subducts into sea.
At the bay, encampment, encampment.
Dispossessed, dispossessed. Sometimes in my mind

ghost Okies still clatter
uphill in ghost Model Ts.
Rosie the Riveters smoke

in postwar sun.
       At the corner, *Happ- Tailor*—
the *y* fallen; hapless.

A lizard runs by.
At the beach yesterday I heard
seven languages; corvid & seal bark.

Last year they tore down
the last town trailer park.
A stream gutters under my house.

A stream follows the path of a faultline.
Our gravestones are signposts to everywhere:
     Yun, Kobayashi, Menendez, Revere.

The Sunset Mausoleum *Welcomes All Visitors.*
          The backhoe inters the arriviste dead.
What's the name of the stream in Huichin Ohlone?

The question lingers. Oyster clouds open.
Our coastlines are swallowed
          are hollowed like vowels—

EMELINE AT SIX WEEKS

You howl, all vowel.
When you babble,

your elocution is clear
as a downhill stream.

With the eyes of a prophet
you gaze beyond us,

and when you cry
your wail is tremendous:

You stage revolution
on behalf of the stars.

UNTITLED WITH SADNESS & SUCKLE

Tonight's emergency
              is not emergent.

      News that stays news but is not a poem.
      Beating. Shooting. Children in cages.

Like when I was at Emily's
      watching cops chase Rodney King.

Same nectarine light.

Sometimes I think that all
privilege is
              is some safer vantage

for watching the trauma, America, happen.
What human words will I use to explain?

In the dream I am screaming:

      My daughter is asking me *why*?
      Now the baby she is

              squalls awake & I haul

myself out to offer   suckle
oxytocin   provisional safety—

we are animal
in the broken ecosystem

      her head smells like milk on my breast

TRAIN THROUGH COLMA

But will anyone teach
the new intelligence to miss
the apricot trees

that bloomed each spring
along these tracks?
Or the way afternoons

blazed with creosote
& ponderosa?
Spring evenings flare

with orange pixels
in the bay-scented valley.
Where in the algorithm

will they account for
the rippling ponies
that roamed outside Fremont?

When the robots have souls,
will they feel longing?
When they feel longing,

will they write poems?

IV

We wrote this book for those friends who want to learn a bit about the geologic foundations of their surroundings . . . we avoided the more rarified topics that only geologists enjoy.

We did our best to avoid crossing the delicate line that separates simplification from oversimplification.

—Roadside Geology of Northern California

RAW NOTES FOR A POEM NOT YET WRITTEN

—San Pablo Ave., El Cerrito, CA

I walk by the
                        Japanese
                                    ruins
gated
                        behind
cracked pavement lot
                                    where the bare hills
        "a riot of poppies"
                                                    frame
little sh
                                    wild lupine

                                    geranium

                                    hothouse thorns

                                    They ~~never~~ came back

their white neighbor ~~saved~~

                                                    (not all)

of their business

                                in the windows
                                            torn rice paper

half a Shinto shrine

Sixty years later
                        toppled
                                    ~~where~~ *they were taken*

last of those buildings

            down   in

                                  O my town.

We perch on

                what was done here.

My best friend's grandmother

                my   first   boyfriend's   grandmother

I knew it later

                they ~~never~~ spoke of it—*(to me)*—

whiskey crates

                                & damp mold

of abandoned places

                Coyote bush rattles: seems

to be asking

            who will they take next

                        ~~when~~ *are they coming?*

ONCE AGAIN AT NONVIOLENCE TRAINING, 2017

Because the white supremacists are coming
because the threat

because   Charlottesville
& if you don't who will

& you never know what baton what chemical
we are marching.

We plan chants.
Make signs at church.

Large assembly: bodies, linoleum, soup.
Cardboard & markers & salt fog drifting.

We bear forward our fury and sorrow.
Estuary sanctuary room for our hope lights.

HATE IS TOXIC TO ALL LIVING CREATURES.
Shalom, salaam. We root our anger.

Are alive together.
Must now be shields to one another.

& John said: *Be a witness.*
We brace one another. Plant our feet.

In fog, promise
to stay together.

We will not raise our hands. We are not leaving.

LOMA PRIETA, 1989

then in chorus up the risers rose
        & for a moment we were riding

high & tottering on the bareback crust.
                   We were girls

preparing for our concert
so even when the raw ground buckled

& bucked us up we went on singing.
Our conductor led us into the courtyard

& in four parts we sang a poem by e. e. cummings
even as we learned that all around us

whole neighborhoods & a freeway had collapsed.
Baudelaire wrote under von Haussmann

that a city's form is always changing
faster than the longings of a mortal heart.

As the sharp quake kicked our lungs
we learned again & for the first time what

it is to live on things
bound to collapse. Later I'd read

Roadside Geology of Northern California
funny yellowing book my father treasured:

I'd learn *rift zone   subduction   slab pull*—
Then as October dusk drew down we sang

although the very bridge
that was our pathway home had sandwiched

between its decks a man a fleet of cars.
Later I watched dismantled piece by piece

the last of those 1930s girders—
week by week torn down as I assembled

the cells of a new daughter in my body.
That night as upthrust settled

we sang on, still children
alive inside the music's oxygen. Even in the face

of devastation
we must make art: This was the lesson

Beth Avakian offered then
without a way of knowing

how much it would mean to me
these years later. In the space

the freeway was, is bay.
                              The new bridge glitters.

They named the quake *Loma Prieta*,
which means '*dark hill*'—

it represents a great collapsing,
though in my heart & memory

it now leans toward song—

SONG IN WHICH WE YET SIDESTEP DISASTER

for Taylor

Even stars are formed by loss. You know
        astronomers believe that galaxies are forged
                out of huge collapsing stars—

hollow, imploding on themselves.
        As stars die the very charge
                of their collapse sets matter loose:

This lost energy becomes a splatter
        of elemental goo spinning in space.
                If this is hard to see, think of a tub,

the one our kids play in each night.
        When it drains, the energy that's lost
in gravity's huge suck is turned to sound. Sound:

what lost force becomes. Sound:
        the gurgle left behind by entropy.
                Think: collapsing stars

forging a galactic paint
        of elements & energy;
                nickel, copper, iron, ore

of which each new world is made.
        Our life is splattered star.
                Or, my love, we're spun of losses.

Is this why
        we sit up on the shore
                & hear the ocean smash the rocks?

The air rings with lost force we call the waves.
　　Ten years ago I gave my life to you,
　　　　& lost some of the life I had before.

We marked promises & gave
　　each other mined-up core
　　　　to wear a while, minted now as rings.

Guise of permanence, to enclose a life.
　　I also know that when I write tonight
　　　　I only chase the pattern that I hear.

Something I meant spins farther off.
　　And: You didn't die that awful year.
　　　　I haven't lost you yet.

My love, I count the lucky stars.
　　I lie, rocking on your breath.

ELK AT TOMALES BAY

Nimble, preserved together,
milkweed-white rears upturned,

female tule elk
bowed into rustling foxtails.

Males muscled over the slopes,
jostling mantles, marking terrain.

Their antlers clambered wide,
steep as open gorges.

As they fed, those branches twitched,
sensory, delicate,

yet as one buck reared his head
squaring to look at us

his antlers & his gaze
held suddenly motionless.

       Further out, the skeleton.
The tar paper it seemed to lie on

was hide.
       Vertebrae like redwood stumps.

In an uneven heart-shaped cavern
       a coccyx curled to its tip.

Ribs fanned open,
       hollow, emptied of organs.

In the bushes, its skull:
sockets & mandible,

sinuses, loose teeth.
All bare now except

that fur the red brown color
of a young boy's head & also

of wild iris stalks in winter
still clung to the drying scalp.

Below the eye's rim sagged
      flat as a bicycle tire.

The form was sinking away.
The skin loosened, becoming other,

shedding the mask that hides
but must also reveal a creature.

Off amid cliffs & hills
some unfleshed force roamed free.

In the wind, I felt
the half-life I watched watch me.

Elk, I said, I see
you abandon this life, this earth.

I stood for a time with the bones.

ETYMOLOGY WITH TECTONIC PLATES

i
Faultline we say & what is this but tendril

> *to fault to foul a falling short a failing*
> > > *to blame to blemish*
> > *e.g. a damaged place*

the word also making visible
> at least in part the unimaginable
moving plate: Earthskull

> > > > > where it buckles

> *to trip to falter err or blunder:*
> > *boundary*
> > *in continuity*
> > *or stone*

Fault we say hiking chert and basalt,

cracked seafloor
under fog.

ii

Later I

rework these lines, chart
lost pangeas, worlds

emerging at the brink   or try

to trace the crevices of mind
to sort

what rubble   all the shift
made visible

linen thread or cord

e.g. also the spool or snare

the mark or stroke or way of making bare

the stave   *to order*

to trace esp. a band or furrow
the measure of a verse or hymn
to bound

to limn

to lineate   *a song*

in a harsh climate
to crack

to realign

SONG WITH WILD PLUM & THORN

The morning is cold & the world is hard
but even in fog it is still midsummer.

The kids need to play & the grocery budget
            ticks toward nothing the way

            the world tips towards doomsday.
The walls in my chest will not let me breathe

& all the screens flicker & still answer nothing, so
            I take the children down to the bike path,

& with buckets & a few blessed hours
        wander a corridor of weedy fruit.

Blackberry, wild plum, all overhung:
        we leaners or gleaners half-acrobatic

lost among boughs—alone till I notice
        others stopping

with buckets or tiffins
        in many languages

        along these tracks picking
        what weeds we still hold in common

        as dry heat builds
and fog thins.   *In common, in common—*

the thought feels strangely radical,
        crumb or bloom beyond

loneliness. For a while, I feel
entirely animal, little forager

                        hungry for fruit.
Black sparkle, pale pit & thorn—

           weeds binding
some world together.

         A word appears in my mind
            holdfast hold fast—

                             sprout—raw volunteer—

for a while it is hand to mouth & to bucket
breathing   *—still here still here—*

AUBADE WITH FAULTLINE & BROKEN PIPE

& when at night there is an earthquake
& in the morning the upended gutter

flows out through the broken mouth of sidewalk
                              & the freed stream splays & loosens

asphalt & Key Route grows impassable; when
            this muddy torrent now recalls

the way in marches   we the people
                do reroute the streets, I remember

        how the pressures exerted
by earthforce are continual & invisible,

        how eruptions   are instantiation.
        Bataille believed *the sacred lies in interruption*

the festival tent unloosed & flapping

after the hurricane

            what hurricane   *what interruption*

                            in an epoch of pressure
unburied water claims its path

                        a force acquires

a voice
            a valence
                        also: It sings as it goes

AUBADE WITH REDWOOD

If we were to go
    if the house fell in an earthquake

if fire, if fire
        & we were burned out

I imagine the redwood
      in what we call our

backyard
      would keep living.

I call myself *I*
      but below its bigness am
small
    eye & animal
      near forest fractal.

Look: The gash
      in its bark
      thickens to heal
         on our neighbor's fence.

Look: The green hummingbirds
      take us as neighbors.

I GAVE MY LOVE A STORY

Now it is night again, child on my chest.
I croon & my song drifts you towards rest.

As I chant in darkness you are also learning
to hear minor scales chime & fourths falling.

Together we hover inside a melody
many dead mothers once sung before.

Tonight *the cherry still has no stone.*
Tonight I rock you out of bodily memory

& these songs are older than we are,
& this tune I hum is wise as a virus;

it makes me a vector
for rhythm & cadence—

(tonight *the chicken still has no bone*):
The song lives on, persists & persists—

PUNCTUATIONS & WIND

Then once again someone is shot
        at a school by a sniper by police in a movie theater
& the many homeless

are hustled & hunted.
        You read how your clothes are sewn by slaves
your dinner fished by slaves

your fruit picked by starving children.
        Mostly you don't get away.
Mostly you raise the children you have,

        afraid of no health care, of losing
        the one goodish job you've finally got.
        Mostly you keep your nose to the grindstone.

Your heart flails
        a thick fish in your throat.
You have felt for a long time that someone is watching:

The administration is eroding your benefits.
        But you are lucky, so you try to feel lucky.
By the numbers you have always lived

in an apartheid state.
        You look at your child.
Read reports of the tear gas.

Text a friend. Cry at night.
        Some days you march when people are marching
some batter windows   some are hit

things are cancelled:

                              The year has been dry
even small rain will lead to mudslides.

Some nights you wake only to feel
          yourself for a few minutes grieving
or praying & hearing in darkness

the old tree tossing & tossing & wild

                              the storm coming

IN OLEMA

February: Buckeye unscissor new leaves.

Cows pasture, buffleheads paddle,

a kestrel perches on a bishop pine.

Now just above us the mountain's humped spine

       pushes north to Alaska.

Extinct invertebrates ride sea cliffs through time.

Even these stones have lost cousins in Mexico.

Even this freshet is landmass torn open,

even these rocks are reft from each other.

       Each shelf pulses onward, a restless swimmer

looking for land though nothing is still.

Gray whales swim through ocean explosions,

along continents forged of cracked dispossession.

Sunset today: The ridges grow luminous.

Sharp air, dark spice: horses exhaling.

They stomp on the cold, steaming, visible earth.

We heat the stove. The children are napping.

The cabin's the raft on which we are floating.

Below us the crust is molten, is nationless.

We only light our lamps on the rift.

V

ENVOI: SAN FRANCISCO

A number of the ships, wharves, and other infrastructure of San Francisco's
Gold Rush waterfront lie buried beneath the streets, sidewalks . . .
—Gold Rush Port: The Maritime Archaelogoy of San
Francisco's Waterfront

City of shipwrecks. City of water.
    Sand hills where mountain lions

prowled above windjammers.
    City whose first Anglo historians proclaimed

themselves to be the only modern *progress*
    & promised to "sweep away *forerunners*"—

who wanted to bind the world's many peoples
    & with their new port to do China

"what the British had done with India
                    (*but sooner*)."

City of Gold Rush & bust & boom,
    city of mudflat, of private wharves.

Buildings to ships, ships into buildings;
        forest to everything;

city of old growth & redwood pilings.
    City of whores & Mackinaw blankets,

of Irish whiskey & fireproof paint,
    of schooners abandoned for goldfields

the Niantic   the Apollo   the General Harrison.
    City whose abandoned ships became

floating opium dens next to floating prisons.
   City of otter pelts & shovel salesmen,

whose white settlers funded their own microgenocides;
   city of quick fires & tallow & opium,

of murre eggs stolen off the Farallones—
   City of landfill & movable real estate

where right now a woman in underwear
   howls in the street

& a barefoot teenager
scratches his sores

   & an addict begged the last of my rice
just outside this room where I am writing

   city of faultline city of water:
        As much as of anywhere I am of you.

NOTES

The town of El Cerrito, California, lies along the Hayward Fault.

The former Contra Costa Florist's shop on San Pablo Avenue in El Cerrito, established in 1934 in the offices of a former quarry company, was run by the Mabuchi family, who during World War II were interned first at the Tanforan Park Racetrack in San Mateo before being relocated to the Topaz internment camp in central Utah.

Portola Middle School in El Cerrito, California, was built in a landslide zone but has since been torn down and rebuilt elsewhere. It has also been renamed Korematsu Middle School to commemorate Fred Toyosaburo Korematsu, who fought in the courts against internment. On December 18, 1944, in a 6–3 decision authored by Justice Hugo Black, the US Supreme Court held that compulsory removal of the Japanese to internment camps, though constitutionally suspect, was justified during circumstances of "emergency and peril."

The poem "Raw Notes for a Poem Not Yet Written" is for Roberto Santiago and Jasmine Hyman.

At the 2017 Centennial of El Cerrito, California, descendants of the original Spanish heirs to the Castro land grant were invited to march in the town's parade.

The town of Olema, California, lies along the San Andreas Fault.

The city of Albany, California, has filed a petition to remove the white cross from Albany Hill.

In 1956, the Castro home burned, creating space for the El Cerrito Plaza. The individuals who set fire to the 1839 adobe house were never prosecuted.

BIOGRAPHICAL NOTE

Tess Taylor's chapbook, *The Misremembered World*, was selected by Eavan Boland for the Poetry Society of America's inaugural chapbook fellowship. The *San Francisco Chronicle* called her first book, *The Forage House*, "stunning," and it was a finalist for the Believer Poetry Award. Her second book, *Work & Days*, was called "our moment's Georgic" by critic Stephanie Burt and named one of the ten best books of poetry of 2016 by the *New York Times*. Taylor's work has appeared in *Atlantic*, *Kenyon Review*, *Poetry*, *Tin House*, the *Times Literary Supplement*, *CNN*, and the *New York Times*. She has received awards and fellowships from MacDowell, Headlands Center for the Arts, and The International Center for Jefferson Studies. Taylor is the on-air poetry reviewer for NPR's *All Things Considered* and has taught at UC Berkeley, St. Mary's University, and Whittier College. She served as Distinguished Fulbright US Scholar at the Seamus Heaney Centre in Queen's University Belfast and was recently the Anne Spencer Poet-in-Residence at Randolph College. Her book *Last West* was released by MoMA books in 2020, and was part of the exhibition *Dorothea Lange: Words & Pictures*. She grew up and lives again in El Cerrito, California.